BUYING

D1366008

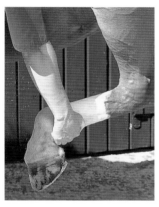

CONTENTS

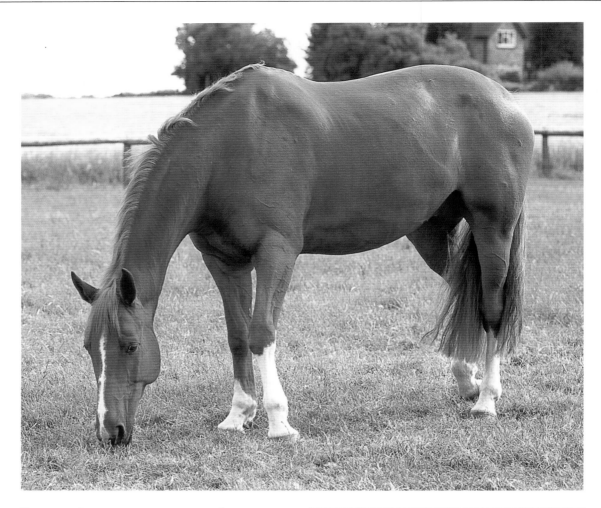

Buying a horse is an exercise with many possible pitfalls and the law demands that buyers know what they are doing. This means that any prospective buyer must get advice where needed as there is no point ending up in court.

Take the gelding shown above. On the face of it, he looks a perfect type of riding horse, big, strong, bold and good looking. But would he be too lively for you, or might he have a temperament problem or a vice that might cause him to be unrideable or a permanent nuisance? And how can you tell if he is sound in eye, heart, wind and limb? How do you tell his age? How can you be sure he is what he's said to be?

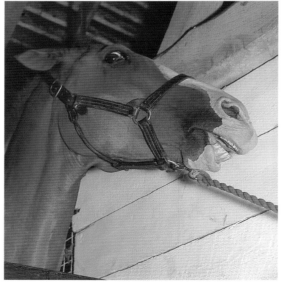

WHERE TO BUY

Depending on what type of horse you want, you go to the source. There are sales for virtually every kind of animal, from Welsh ponies to Thoroughbreds. But if you do not feel competent to buy in the hussle and bustle of a sale, then try the advertisements of your local paper, or a horsey magazine, or a computer database that specialises in this line of business. You could also approach a local dealer or horseperson, as 'word of mouth' leads to many sales.

THE HORSE YOU NEED WILL BE:

- of the right size and strength to carry your weight;
- of an age that promises a reasonable life-span with every prospect of staying sound;
- able to handle the discipline for which he is required.

YOUR RIGHTS AND DUTIES

- Buyers of goods in Britain are protected by the Sale of Goods Act (1979) and by the amendments of 1994.
- This is a pathway to legal redress if there is a complaint.
- Your protection is the care you take, the diligence with which you approach the exercise.

- A buyer has no redress if failing to see obvious problems.
- Ignorance is not a plea that will be accepted.
- A vendor will not be obliged to reimburse you if inexperience prevented your knowing the horse was unsound.

DUE CARE

It is vital to inspect an animal first and see any evident defects. Take this selection here. The bump below the knee (*see right*) on the inside of the leg is a splint; it could be bigger than this or so small it is barely visible. A noticeable splint would be a blemish if you wanted a show horse.

The fetlock on the chestnut leg (*below left*) is badly deformed from injury. Would you see it if at a sale with no experienced help?

The white tendons have both been injured (*below right*). If you bought the horse like this you could not return him. He is, however, a perfectly good hunter gelding and does not suffer any ill effects from these legs but they affect his value and might jeopardise his chances of racing.

THE SELLER'S LEGAL DUTY

- The seller must declare any known material information that might influence future usefulness.
- This does not include faults or blemishes that are self-evident.
- It does include anything you cannot see that is relevant, including temperament and vice.

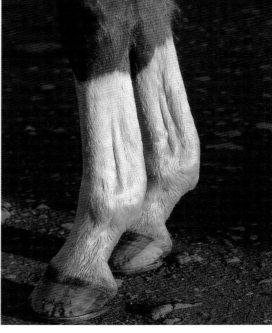

INTENDED USE

Be clear in your mind exactly what you are aiming for. If it is a first horse, you do not want to go to a Thoroughbred sale and buy a racehorse you will not be able to handle.

If, on the other hand, you intend to ride a lot and hope to progress to competition, you want an animal that will be able to take you there.

WHERE TO GET ADVICE

If you lack knowledge and wish to buy a horse to race, jump or event, which you will not ride or train yourself, you then rely fully on the opinion of others. An agent may pick an animal and buy it, with your approval, and you are guided by the quality of this advice.

If the horse is required for racing, an agent who specialises in racing will advise on breeding and form. Make sure you get a sound animal that can race and, if for steeplechasing, jump.

Other agents and dealers will find almost any type of horse or pony you seek. Get the special advice of a vet if you are faced with a specific lesion like the splint, fetlock and tendon injuries mentioned before. Get more than one opinion if you are in doubt.

VETERINARY EXAMINATION

Veterinary examination of a horse before buying is a safeguard encouraged by virtually all agents and trainers. Your new horse can generally be insured from the moment a certificate is issued. The vet will examine the eyes, heart, wind and action and will provide information you will not otherwise have access to.

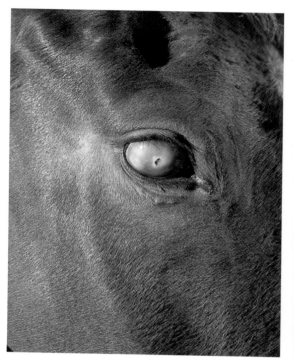 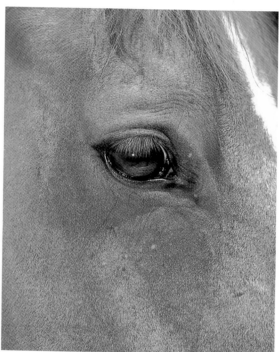

The eye lesion on the dark horse is self-evident, but can you be sure that the eye of the chestnut is perfect? It might have an early cataract.

Any defect found will be discussed with you. Something that may not intrude on your proposed use, like the old scar here (*right*), you may decide to ignore. The vet may say it is not significant. Alternatively, there may be doubt. An X-ray might be needed but you would not have the option to X-ray at a sale, in which case you would have the right to reject the animal from the outset. Perhaps you require another opinion? At a public sale, all will depend on the exact conditions of sale which are normally printed in the catalogue. Be sure to read them.

In a private sale, the examination is carried out once a horse has been seen and an agreement to buy has been made.

On the certificate, it will be declared that an animal is suitable (or not) for the purpose for which you wish to use it. If a horse is to be ridden, to jump, perhaps to be driven, it must have the potential to carry out these tasks, and the vet will be your judge in deciding it. It is vital this opinion is written on your certificate as it might be worthless without it.

Examination may well be the basis of any complaint you have. It can be a false economy not to have it done, and an examination at a later date may fail to establish that a given problem existed at the time you bought.

VETTING AT SALES

Facilities are usually provided for vetting within the sales complex but there may be a time limit, which it is vital to respect. Alternatively, buyers may be given time to take an animal away to be vetted and the existence of this facility should be listed in the conditions of sale. Rejected animals must be returned within the specified time. You may require more than one opinion.

THE VET WORKS FOR YOU

- Use an independent vet who does not work for the seller and does not know the animal.
- The examination is a contract between you and the vet, and it is you, the buyer, who pays.
- If further tests are needed, these will have to be agreed by the vendor, and are also at your expense.
- The sale is not completed until all problems are discussed with you and you are satisfied.
- A horse cannot be rejected for frivolous reasons – like something you failed to see before bidding.
- Remember the vet is not providing a guarantee, but an expert opinion of an animal at the time it is examined.
- There are conditions, like vices, which may not be detected.
- The vendor's disclosure of these is paramount.

CONFORMATION

To be a good judge of conformation takes years of observation but good conformation is related to soundness. While there are always exceptions, poor conformation can inhibit performance and increase the chances of unsoundness. It is, therefore, best to avoid horses with evident anatomical faults unless you know exactly what you are doing. Good conformation is aligned to good action and may be associated with ability. It is what appeals to judges in show rings.

THE HEAD AND NECK

The head contains the eyes, ears, nostrils and mouth, also the brain, all vital structures which need to be functionally sound. The long neck has great scope of movement, up and down and to each side. Together, the head and neck must be in balance with the rest of the body, moving freely and without impediment through all gaits.

HEAD AND NECK FAULTS

- If the head is too big, the animal may be unbalanced.
- A ewe neck is unsightly and could limit movement in jumping.
- Scars to the mouth, nostrils, eyes and ears are all capable of causing problems.
- Tear-staining can indicate eye infection or blockage of the draining duct.
- Swelling between the jaws might mean infection.
- Tumours are common in the throat of grey-coated animals.
- Check for missing or rotten teeth.
- Restrictions of movement in the head and neck are best noted when an animal is moving through its gaits.

THE FORELIMB

Because of the anatomical design of the horse's forelimb, the bony structures up to and including the knee are exposed to the greatest proportion of stress.

The feet The feet must be well made, of a size to support the horse's weight, and match one another. The grey horse has a corrective shoe for a fault you might not see from a side view but it can be seen from the front. The hind view shows a 'buttress' foot.

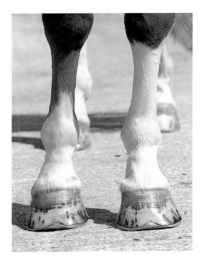

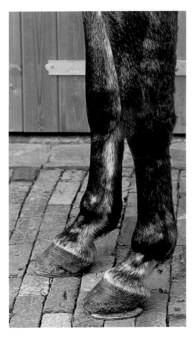

FOOT FAULTS

- Flat soles bruise easily and predispose to lameness.
- Small feet create shoeing problems that might prevent the horse being ridden.
- A horse might have special shoes to relieve lameness.
- After laminitis, concentric rings appear on the hoof wall.
- A contracted foot is smaller than its fellow and the frog is shrunken; the horse is not sound and its value is affected.
- Sidebones are bony prominences at the level of the coronet on either side; they cause lameness, though horses with fully formed sidebones may well remain sound.
- Low ringbone is a serious bony enlargement at the level of the coronet tending to surround the top of the hoof.
- Buttress foot is a similar condition to low ringbone affecting the front of the foot only.

The pastern The pastern runs from the coronet to the fetlock. It should continue the line of the hoof at an angle of 45–50 degrees for the forelimb, or 50–55 degrees for a hind limb. Expect a non-Thoroughbred to be more upright and, perhaps, to have shorter pasterns.

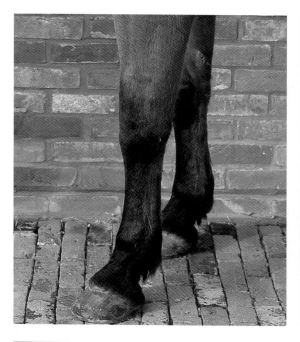

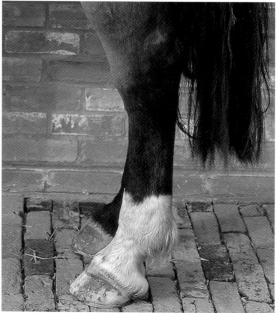

PASTERN FAULTS

- If the pastern angle is too upright, bony structures may be injured.
- If too sharply angled, the ligaments are weakened.
- The angle is changed when the heels are too low or too high.
- Excessively long light-boned pasterns are innately weak.
- High ringbone occurs in the middle of the pastern and is a serious bony enlargement that surrounds the pastern joint.
- Lameness is usual with ringbone, though there are exceptions.

The fetlock The fetlock joint is set between the pastern and cannon and is vital for support and movement. At the back of the joint, two small sesamoid bones help the movement of the tendons and provide attachment for many important ligaments. The strength of the fetlock is also affected by the angulation of the limb.

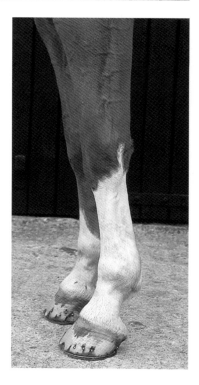

The joints on the legs of the chestnut with the white stockings (*right*) are upright, though strong and unblemished and in no way do they weaken the horse.

The chestnut legs here, on the other hand, are lighter boned, with proportionally longer pasterns and cannons, and are likely to be weaker. There is a difference in age between the two horses and the three-year-old chestnut filly will have time to grow more bone.

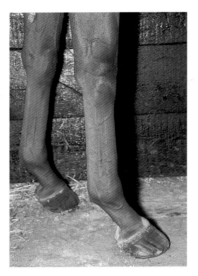

FETLOCK FAULTS

- Windgalls are seen as fluid swellings at the upper rear of the joint, between the tendons and the bone.
- Fluid within the joint itself might be caused by a sprain.
- Bony enlargement of the joint rim may indicate degenerative changes.
- Heat may result from recent injury and is always significant.

The cannon The cannon is the long bone between the fetlock and the knee. It is an area subject to considerable concussion, especially on hard ground. Its strength depends on its stage of maturity as well as the amount of bone; bone does not mature fully until a horse is four to five years old.

The black foreleg is that of a mature horse showing a splint below the knee. The chestnut hind cannon is long and weak and shows a slightly bucked shin.

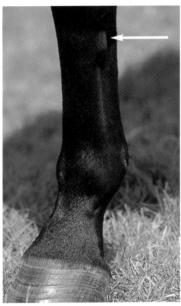

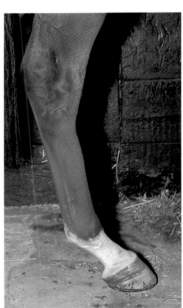

CANNON FAULTS

- Young animals with too little bone are prone to injury.
- When even light bone is fully matured, there is less trouble.
- The junction of the cannon bone with the small splint bones is the seat of splints, mostly on the inside of the limb.
- Splints can be single or multiple and vary from the size of a pea to a walnut on front or hind limbs.
- Sore shins often mean minute fractures that may cause bilateral lameness. Affected horses will flinch to hand pressure on the front of the cannon.
- Bucked shins are bony thickenings at the front of the cannon, resulting from chronic sore shins.

The tendons The two flexor tendons and the suspensory ligament are situated at the back of the cannon. These are vital support structures and tendons are the continuations of muscles in the upper limb to their connections below. On the leg shown here, the superficial and deep flexor tendons appear as one structure at the back; the suspensory ligament stands out between them and the bone.

TENDON FAULTS

- Fresh injury is marked by swelling, heat and pain.
- Old injuries cause distortion of surface anatomy but are cold and only an expert may detect the swelling.
- Any sign of injury is significant and may affect value.
- An old healed injury might not affect a hunter.
- Recently injured tendons, without swelling, but hot and painful to the hand, are likely to break down if the horse is ridden.
- The suspensory ligament rests between the flexor tendons and the bone, it thickens when strained.

The knee The knee comprises seven (sometimes eight) small bones formed in two rows between the cannon below and the radius and ulna above. It is very important to the support of the limb and body and to movement.

Viewed from the side, the knee should be perfectly straight between forearm and cannon, as with this yearling here.

From the front, the knees should neither converge or diverge. The chestnut horse's legs converge slightly when judged against a straight line drawn up from the ground. He is, however, a mature racehorse with no major blemishes, and the condition is exaggerated by the fact that he needs shoeing. The bay is showing slightly the opposite effect. Both faults are most serious in immature horses.

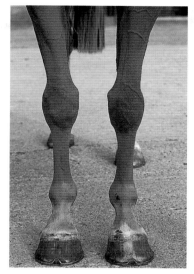

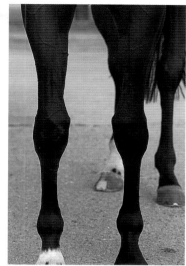

KNEE FAULTS

- Backward inclination of the knee is a serious fault that often leads to lameness.
- Forward inclination is unsightly but less significant.
- Bench knees are off-set from the front and the condition is most serious in young animals.
- Scars are common and should be judged on how they restrict movement.
- Hard bumps that restrict movement are potentially serious and might need to be X-rayed to gauge their significance.
- Fluid swellings over the knee are unsightly and may, or may not, inhibit performance; take advice if in doubt.
- Pain may cause stumbling on hard or uneven surfaces, or when landing from a jump.

The upper forelimb The bony structures from the knee upwards are not so frequently injured but elbow and shoulder lameness occurs and muscular and ligamentous injuries are common. A strong forearm should run into a full and well-formed shoulder with an angulation to parallel that of the pastern.

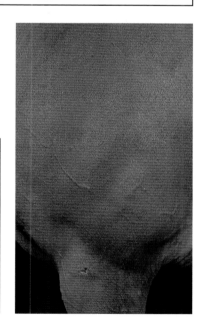

UPPER LIMB FAULTS

- Heat and swelling of the elbow and shoulder joints occur.
- Bursitis may cause a soft swelling at the front of the shoulder joint.
- Fistulous withers have a pustular discharge with open sores on the top and side of the withers.
- Muscular injuries will change the flight of an affected limb.
- Observe the horse's action from in front and from the side.
- Swelling or wasting of affected muscles may be seen.

THE RIBCAGE AND FLANK

The ribcage accommodates the heart and lungs, two essential organs for competition animals. The flank and lower abdomen may contain surgical scars and these could be very significant. Sections of bowel may have been removed and the animal may have special dietary considerations because of this. This information would be vital in a sale and a seller might well be at fault if failing to divulge it.

THE BACK AND LOINS

The back and loins are critical, primarily because they carry the rider's weight. The back has to be strong and adequately mus-cled. The loins are the muscular connection of the back to the pelvis; they cover the lumbo-sacral junction which is pivotal in back movement and they need to be strong and well-developed to serve this function. Long backs are potentially weak.

Roach-backed horses can be uncomfort-able to ride but there is no inherent weak-ness in this type of conformation. This

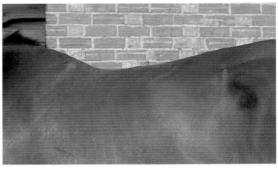

roach-backed horse has had problems with his saddle but he is a good racehorse who suffers no more than other horses with back problems.

The pelvis of the grey horse is dropping badly on one side; compare this pelvis with the perfect round shape of the quarters on the chestnut.

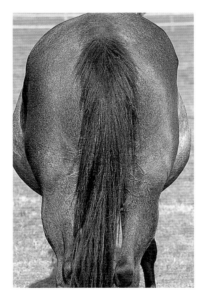
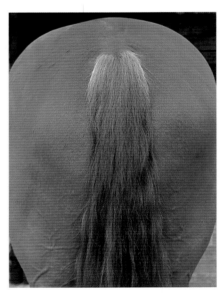

BACK AND LOIN FAULTS

- Evident lesions like saddle sores, cysts and warbles can prevent a horse from being ridden.
- Lameness, or change of action, originating from back pain is common and can prove limiting.
- Asymmetry of the back and quarters is best seen from behind. The significance can be best judged when the horse is walked and trotted, in a straight line, away and back.
- Symptoms may get worse under saddle and with the weight of a rider.

THE HIND LIMB

The hind limbs are the powerhouse of all forward movement. They must, therefore, show no evident stress to the structures that bend as they propel the body.

The lower hind limb needs the same good conformation as the forelimb, except for the more upright stance through the pastern.

The hocks The hocks must be strong and well made. They should not be too upright and there should be no weakness in the way they unite with the cannon below, or the gaskin above, and no undue tendency to angle inwards or outwards when viewed from behind.

The hock on the bay horse is slightly capped but there is a good straight line down the back of the leg from the point of the hock to the fetlock. The hocks of the chestnut deviate slightly outwards but they are the sound hocks of a good jumper and the fact they are unblemished is a sign of their strength.

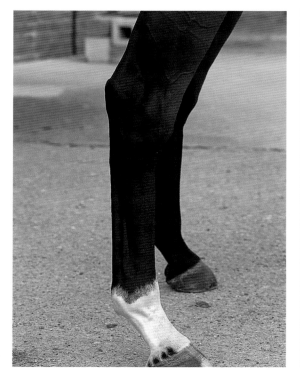

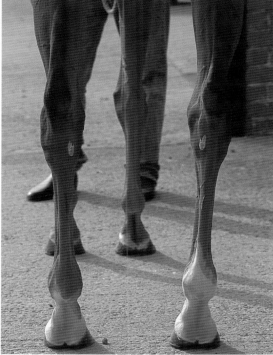

The bay shown here, taken from an oblique angle, shows the prominent head of a splint bone intruding on the downward line from the point of the hock, known as a false curb.

A flexion, or spavin test is useful for assessing the significance of hock conditions.

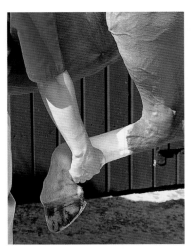

HOCK FAULTS

- Curbs are unsightly blemishes at the back of the joint that are particularly unwanted when showing.
- Curbs can result from a weakness at the point where the hock meets the cannon at the back of the leg.
- Bone spavin is a hardened enlargement at the inner lower aspect of the hock and is a cause of lameness.
- Bog spavin is an increase of fluid in the joint and is seen as soft swellings at the front and to either side behind the hock.
- Thoroughpin consists of two soft swellings in the hollow above and at the back of the hock.
- A sprung hock is swollen all over.
- Any of these blemishes are potentially serious.

The stifle, hip and pelvis The stifle is a complex joint at the upper end of the gaskin, or second thigh, and is similar to the human knee. The patella, equivalent to the knee-cap, sits at the front of the stifle. Dense muscle surrounds the femur, that runs between the stifle and hip. The hip joint is strong, deep seated, and not that frequently injured. The pelvis is where the hind limb is attached to the body through the hip. The sacrum forms the roof of the pelvis and is the means through which the pelvis is attached to the spine.

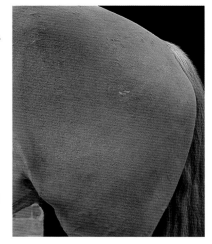

WARNING

Poor conformation might provide a good excuse for avoiding a particular horse but a vet examining the animal may not be entitled to reject it unless there is lameness or unless there inevitably will be in time. If you have inspected an animal and agreed to buy subject to the vet's opinion, you may be obliged to proceed even when the defect is drawn to your attention.

STIFLE, HIP AND PELVIS FAULTS

- An upright stifle may lead to upward displacement of the patella, which might need surgery.
- Fluid in the stifle is abnormal and means the horse is unsound.
- The hip joint may be involved in pelvic fractures which would cause severe lameness.
- The upper pelvic region is a common site of muscle and bone disturbance.
- The outer angle of the ilium is commonly injured by being struck on doorposts.

THE ACTION

It is vital to see a horse through all its gaits before buying and, when in doubt, get advice. See the horse walk and trot in a straight line towards you and away from you. Ask for it to be turned sharply to either side and to move backwards. Have it lunged or ridden to see its faster gaits. You might see it in the field where freedom of movement and absence of pain would be shown by the horse 'letting off steam' as the bay is doing here.

SPECIAL SYSTEMS

THE SKIN

Warts, melanomas, sarcoids and other growths may all be found on the skin. Undeclared melanomas and sarcoids would warrant the rejection of an animal and it is important to get a professional opinion if in doubt. The photos here show a number of melanomas, a sarcoid and a sweet-itch lesion, any of which are of major significance when buying.

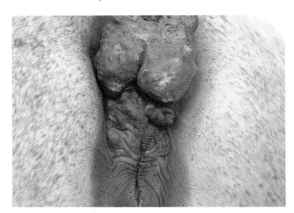

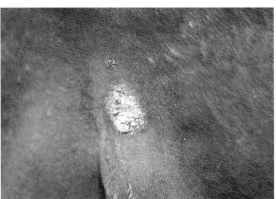

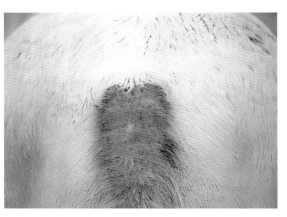

WARNING

- Melanomas are cancers and should be seen as such.
- Sarcoids may be very troublesome.
- A horse with an undeclared sarcoid can usually be returned.
- Sweet-itch can be a persistent problem.
- Do not handle or buy horses with ringworm lesions.
- Do not buy horses with open discharges or infections; some, like strangles, are highly contagious.

THE EYES

Any visible surface lesion may interfere with vision, but deeper conditions will only be seen by a vet using an opthalmascope. It is important to take advice.

Observable lesions of the cornea, cataracts, scars and tear-staining are all significant conditions.

THE RESPIRATORY SYSTEM

A sound respiratory system is essential in any athlete or competing animal. Conditions of the larynx may inhibit the inflow of air, while conditions of the lungs may prevent normal exchange of gases between the blood and the air. See the horse in his stable and note any wheezing or coughing. In order to examine the respiratory system fully, a horse must be lunged or ridden.

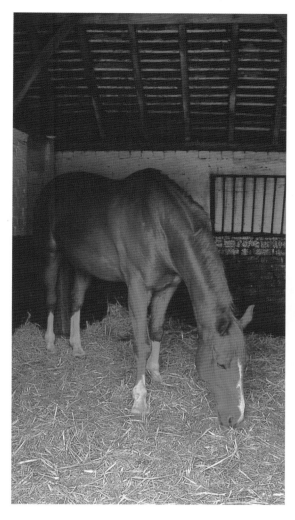

RESPIRATORY FAULTS

- Problems with the larynx may cause inspiratory noises when a horse is cantered. Sometimes these result from infection, and endoscopic examination is needed to tell the difference.
- COPD is a chronic lung disease evident by an increased breathing rate and a marked effort to breathe.
- Wind conditions may form specific sale conditions and it is important to know these, especially when buying animals to race or for competition.
- With racing animals, seek a warranty that states that the horse does not suffer from EIPH (exercise induced pulmonary haemorrhage), marked by bleeding from the lungs during a race; affected animals may stop suddenly.

THE HEART

The only way to be sure a horse's heart is sound is to have it examined by an experienced vet. Murmurs and rhythm irregularities have varying significance in relation to performance and it is important to know exactly where you stand. Heart conditions generally affect resale value, often even when an animal is performing well.

TYPE OF HORSE

COLOUR, SEX, AGE AND HEIGHT

It is your duty to be satisfied on all these points before buying. You are expected to see and know the colour and sex of an animal. Be careful that a gelding is not in fact a rig. Look out for inguinal and abdominal hernias.

Be sure to check the authenticity of age claims where there are no supporting documents. Ageing by teeth is, however, an imperfect exercise, with accuracy only possible up to six years. After this, many claims of age are difficult to confirm.

Check the height of a horse you wish to buy, irrespective of what a catalogue might declare. With the exception of ponies with height certificates, horses are seldom taken back because they were the wrong height.

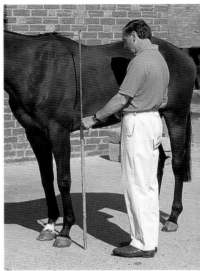

THE BREED

Check all documentation, especially identity charts against the animal presented. Pedigree animals must have proper proof of registration. Whether you want an animal to show, or for something like trotting, this kind of information is essential.

BUYING TO BREED

If you are buying a mare for breeding, it may be important to check her previous breeding record and have a full examination of her reproductive system especially if she is barren, i.e. not had a foal for some time. It also is important to ensure freedom from CEM (contagious equine metritis) and EVA (equine viral arteritis). See if the mare is stitched and avoid any discharges like that shown here.

If buying a stallion, the external reproductive anatomy must be normal. Swabs and blood samples are needed to cover against conditions like CEM and EVA. It is also wise to see a covering and observe the horse's temperament and interest in his mares.

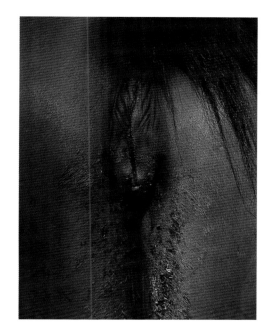

CONDITIONS FOR RETURNING HORSES

- Vices which have not been declared, e.g. crib-biting, wind-sucking, weaving, box-walking.
- Clinical conditions like shivering and wobbling.
- Improper identification, failure to register, improper description; disqualified from racing, etc.
- Undeclared surgery for wind problems, etc.
- The horse is a rig.
- It is a vendor's duty to declare if a horse is denerved or has had any significant surgery that is not evident.
- Any other problem which has not been declared.

USEFUL TIPS

- See every animal you might decide to bid on well in advance.
- Always read the Conditions of Sale with care.
- Check the descriptions in the catalogue and note any warranties or declared problems.
- Always suspect horses sold without a guarantee; you may not be able to return them, even if they are unsound.
- Ask about the stage of training for horses in work.
- Find out what racing or competition entries have been made.
- Be slow to bid on an animal you see for the first time in the sales ring because faults are easily hidden as a horse circles.
- Always inspect any certificates from a vendor, and take advice on these when in doubt about them.
- Do not accept a lame or unsound horse without a warranty.
- In private sales, ask for further tests like scans and X-rays if they seem necessary.

WARRANTIES AND TRIALS

Horses are frequently sold with warranties, for example, a horse with a previous injury might be sold as functionally sound despite the problem. If this proved incorrect, the horse would be returnable under normal circumstances.

Sometimes an extended warranty is given at a sale, or privately, to cover some slight problem. If there is a minor lameness from, say, a lost shoe, the horse could be returned if the lameness persisted beyond a few days. An extended warranty might also be given in order to allow a horse's wind to be properly tested, if this was not done at the time of buying. It is important to establish liability for accidents in these cases, and it is wise to insure against injury, etc.

In private sales, a vendor might agreed a trial period after which a horse could be returned if unsuitable.

VICES

Vices are faults of temperament or habit, which may not show themselves at the time of buying. A vendor must declare them, although some horses might weave briefly only after changing to a new home.

Always get a witnessed verbal or written disclaimer from a vendor that there is no existing vice. This would include vices of temperament that might make a horse unrideable or dangerous to handle.

A vet cannot be expected to detect vices, and will accept no liability on this matter.

The presence of an anti-weaving device might suggest there is a vice, and horses that crib-bite or wind-suck may do so as you watch.

This type of truculent behaviour of rolling in the showring would hardly amount to a vice but it might cause a buyer to be cautious about temperament if the horse was particularly aggressive.

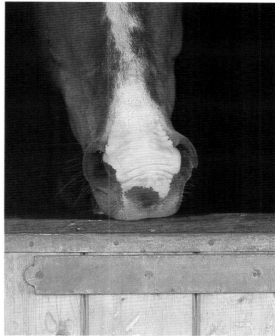

TYPES OF VICE

- A weaver is a horse that habitually swings its head and neck and transfers weight from one fore-foot to the other while in a standing position.
- A box-walker is a horse that walks about its box aimlessly and continually.
- A wind-sucker is a horse that continually swallows air, irrespective of whether this is associated with grasping fixed objects with its incisor teeth or not.
- A crib-biter is a horse that habitually grasps objects, most often wood, with its incisor teeth.
- A shiverer is a horse that shows spasmodic movements of the tail and hind limbs associated with disease of the central nervous system; this is best seen when the horse is moving backwards.
- Stringhalt is an exaggerated lifting of the hind leg when the horse is moving forward.

BLOOD SAMPLES

Finally, it is important to consider that an animal you buy may have been given drugs to mask lameness or some other condition that will become apparent when the effect of the drug has worn off. You can cover yourself against this by asking for blood samples to be taken at completion of the sale.

ACKNOWLEDGEMENTS

My thanks to the following people for facilities and animals provided:
Sharon Baldwin of Meadow Stud and Brendan Paterson BVetMed, Cert
ESM, MRCVS; Patricia Morris and Patrick Conlon of Caddicroft Farm,
Pershore; Michael and Averil Opperman of Tenbury Wells; J.C. Fox of
Marlborough; Mrs. Penelope Glen of Forest Hill, Oxford.
Thanks also to all others whose animals appear in this book.

British Library Cataloguing-in-Publication Data.
A catalogue record for this book is available from the
British Library

ISBN 0.85131.731.6

© J. A. Allen & Co. Ltd. 1999

Published in Great Britain in 1999 by
J. A. Allen & Company Limited,
1 Lower Grosvenor Place, Buckingham Palace Road,
London, SW1W OEL

Design and Typesetting by Paul Saunders
Series editor Jane Lake
Colour Separation by Tenon & Polert Colour Scanning Ltd.
Printed in Hong Kong by Dah Hua Printing Press Co. Ltd.